Cornerstones of Freedom
The Story of

Jefferson Davis

Zachary Kent

 CHILDRENS PRESS ®
CHICAGO

Library of Congress Cataloging-in-Publication Data

Kent, Zachary.
  Jefferson Davis / by Zachary Kent.
    p. cm. — (Cornerstones of freedom)
  A biography of the soldier and statesman who became
the president of the Confederacy during the Civil War.
  ISBN 0-516-06664-1
  1. Davis, Jefferson, 1808-1889—Juvenile literature.
2. Statesmen—United States—Biography—Juvenile
literature. 3. Presidents—Confederate States of
America—Biography—Juvenile literature. [1. Davis,
Jefferson, 1808-1889. 2. Presidents—Confederate States
of America.] I. Title. II. Series.
E467.1.D26K46 1993
973,7´13´092—dc20   92-36894
[B]   CIP
                                                              AC

Hundreds of horsemen galloped from the road and scattered through the woods just north of Irwinville, Georgia. In the early dawn of May 10, 1865, these grim riders charged suddenly toward a small camp of tents and wagons hidden among the trees. Cracking rifle fire and yelling voices awakened fifty-six-year-old Jefferson Davis. Staring through the darkness, he quickly recognized the attacking riders by their blue uniforms.

"Federal cavalry!" he warned his wife, Varina.

After four years of bloody struggle, the American Civil War had reached its end. The Union armies of the northern states had beaten the Confederate armies of the South. Now, regiments of Union cavalrymen scoured the southern countryside, hoping to capture the last of the Confederate leaders.

The Yankee horsemen were surrounding the camp. Varina Davis begged her husband to escape. After a moment's hesitation, Davis grabbed a long rain cape. His wife threw a shawl over his head and shoulders to protect him against the cold and damp. Silently, he stepped from their tent and walked toward a nearby stream. If he could reach the swamp on the other side, perhaps he would be safe. Quickly, Varina Davis gave her maid a bucket and sent her to walk with Mr. Davis. In the dim morning light, it looked as if the two were going to fetch water. Davis's tall, thin form, however, made at least one Federal cavalryman suspicious. Private Andrew Bee rode close and shouted, "Halt!"

Jefferson Davis surrendering to Union troops on May 10, 1865

After his capture, Davis was taken to prison in a horse-drawn Union ambulance.

In an instant, Davis threw off the shawl and cape. "He turned right square around and came towards me fast," remembered Bee. Expecting a fight, the Union soldier raised his rifle. With a frightened scream, Varina Davis rushed to her husband's side. Davis realized that further struggle would be useless. He quietly surrendered. Soon, the Yankee troopers recognized their prisoner. Jefferson Davis was the president of the defeated Confederate States of America. With pride and dignity, he had led the South during four hard years of war. Perhaps more than anyone, Davis symbolized the hopes and stubborn spirit of the Confederacy.

Davis spent a year studying at Transylvania University in Kentucky.

The youngest of ten children, Jefferson Davis was born in present-day Todd County, Kentucky, on June 3, 1808. Two years later, the Davis family moved to Wilkinson County, Mississippi. In this frontier region, Samuel Davis chopped down trees and cleared a farm. Working beside the few black slaves he owned, he planted rows of cotton. Samuel and Jane Davis tried to provide their youngest son with the best possible education. When he was fifteen, Jefferson was sent to study at Transylvania University, a prestigious school in Lexington, Kentucky. The next year, Samuel Davis obtained a United States Military Academy appointment for his son.

In the fall of 1824, young Jeff Davis stepped ashore at the Hudson River landing at West Point, New York. As a military cadet, he soon learned the routine of West Point. Drum rolls shook him awake each dawn. Dressed in his handsome uniform, he marched, drilled, and stood at attention for roll calls and inspections. His classes included such subjects as military history, military tactics, and mathematics. After four years, on June 30, 1828, he graduated twenty-third in a class of thirty-two students.

Commissioned a second lieutenant in the United States Army, Davis journeyed west.

A drawing done by Davis when he was at West Point

An engraving of West Point in the 1800s

Black Hawk

Jefferson Davis at age thirty-two

Between 1829 and 1832, the young officer served at such frontier outposts as Fort Winnebago in the Wisconsin Territory and Fort Crawford in the Michigan Territory. His many duties included buying food for fort kitchens, operating an army sawmill, and pursuing army deserters.

Panic swept the Northwest in 1832. Sauk and Fox Indians led by Chief Black Hawk battled for the right to remain on their traditional Wisconsin homelands. An army of United States soldiers and state militiamen quickly defeated Black Hawk's uprising. It was Lieutenant Davis who escorted Black Hawk and other Indian prisoners by boat down the Mississippi River. Later, Black Hawk called his considerate guard a "good and brave young chief."

Lieutenant Davis was a striking figure at parties and dances. He stood tall and slim, with a strong jawline, piercing blue eyes, and thick brown hair. While at Fort Crawford, Davis fell in love with Sarah Knox Taylor, the daughter of the fort's tough old commander. Colonel Zachary Taylor wished a better future for his daughter than an unsettled army life. He frowned upon her growing romance with Davis. At last, however, Colonel Taylor reluctantly agreed to their marriage. On June 17, 1835, twenty-seven-year-old Jefferson Davis and twenty-one-year-old Sarah Taylor exchanged wedding vows at the home of Sarah's aunt near Louisville, Kentucky.

Brierfield, Jefferson Davis's home before the Civil War

A tooting steamboat carried the happy bride and groom down the Mississippi River. Davis had resigned his army commission with plans to become a Mississippi planter. His wealthy brother Joseph helped him out by giving him eight hundred acres of land at Davis Bend in Warren County, twenty miles south of Vicksburg. Davis named his plantation "Brierfield" and bought black slaves to help him plant a cotton crop. "The country is quite healthy," Sarah wrote to her parents. Unfortunately, she was mistaken. That summer, tragedy struck when Jefferson and Sarah both fell ill with malaria. Davis survived his terrible fever, but Sarah died on September 15, 1835, after just three months of marriage.

The loss of his young wife completely crushed Davis. Full of grief, he continued clearing the land at Brierfield. Sometimes, he rode to Joseph's nearby plantation, called "Hurricane." In his brother's library, he silently read books about law, philosophy, and history. He passed seven lonely years by providing himself with a careful, scholarly education.

In 1843, youthful, bright-eyed Varina Howell met Davis during a Christmas visit to Hurricane.

Jefferson Davis's second wife, Varina Howell Davis

Jefferson and Varina Davis

"He impresses me," she wrote her mother, "as a remarkable kind of man." Smart and lively Varina greatly impressed Jefferson Davis, too. Before long, the couple was engaged. Jefferson Davis married nineteen-year-old Varina on February 26, 1845.

"He is the greatest man for soft words and hard arguments ever listened to," one Mississippi Democrat described Davis in 1844. More and more, Davis was taking an interest in politics. At picnics and barbecues, his fine speeches excited many listeners. In 1845, Mississippi voters

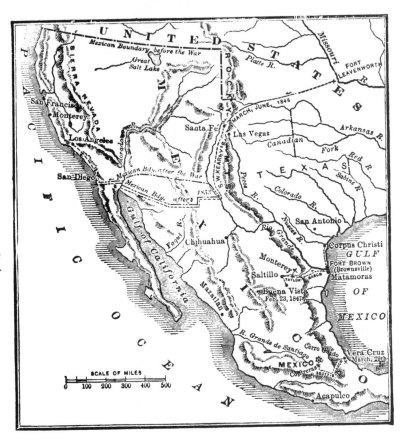

A map of the Mexican War

elected Davis to the United States House of Representatives. Massachusetts congressman John Quincy Adams, former president of the United States, heard an early Davis speech. Impressed by the new congressman, Adams predicted, "We shall hear more of that young man, I fancy."

Before Davis could complete his first term in Congress, however, war erupted with Mexico. For years, the United States had argued with Mexico about where the Texas border line should be. Suddenly, in April 1846, American and Mexican soldiers clashed along the Rio Grande. Congress reacted by swiftly declaring war. "In June 1846,"

Davis later wrote, "a regiment of Mississippi volunteers was organized at Vicksburg, of which I was elected colonel." At the head of this regiment, called the Mississippi Rifles, Colonel Davis marched into Mexico.

As part of an invading American army commanded by Davis's former father-in-law, Zachary Taylor, the Mississippians charged into the Mexican city of Monterrey on September 21, 1846. Bullets loudly rattled on the cobblestones. Men screamed and clutched at wounds. Fearlessly, Colonel Davis led his soldiers forward.

Colonel Jefferson Davis fought bravely in the Battle of Monterrey.

General Zachary Taylor commanding his troops at Buena Vista

Exclaimed one Mississippi Rifleman, "It is to me a wonder that he was not killed, as he was at all times in the hottest of the fight."

After capturing Monterrey, General Taylor continued south. At a ranch called Buena Vista, on February 23, 1847, the American soldiers braced themselves to meet a huge Mexican attack. The hardy Mississippi Riflemen filled one important gap in the line. Joining other regiments, they formed an enormous V, with the open end facing the approaching enemy. "Hold your fire, men, until they get close," Davis shouted, "and then give it to them!" With banners streaming, the lead brigade of Mexican cavalry galloped into the trap. From two sides, the Americans shot scores of lancers from their horses, and the shocked Mexican survivors fled.

Jefferson Davis as a military man

Early in the day, a bullet had struck Davis in the right foot. Despite the pain, he remained in his saddle until sunset and American victory. Jefferson Davis returned home cheered as one of the heroes of the Mexican War. The governor of Mississippi rewarded Davis by appointing him to fill out the term of a United States senator who had died. Still on crutches, he took his oath at the U.S. Capitol on December 6, 1847. After that term expired, he was elected to the Senate in his own right, and ably served there until 1850. During that time, he grew to become the leading senatorial spokesman for the South.

President Franklin Pierce named Davis U.S. secretary of war in 1853. During his term, Davis increased the size of the army from ten thousand to fifteen thousand men. He ordered improvements in uniforms and equipment and supervised the construction of new arsenals and forts. He also introduced the military use of camels in the dry regions of the West. War Department clerk William B. Lee recalled, "He was one of the best secretaries of war that ever served. He was a kind, social man, very considerate, and pleasant to serve under. . . . He

HOEING COTTON

These drawings illustrate the contrast between the economies of the North and South in the mid-1800s.

was a regular bull-dog when he formed an opinion, for he would never let go."

In 1857, Davis once more climbed the steps of the U.S. Capitol, to serve another term as a Mississippi senator. "There is a settled gloom hanging over everyone here," wrote Varina. For many years, the subject of slavery had threatened to tear the nation in two. In the North, where factories thrived, thousands of European immigrants were willing to work for low wages. Most northerners had no use for slavery, and many considered it cruel and immoral. The South, on the other hand, depended upon slavery for the success of its farming economy. In the Senate, Davis's voice rang out in defense of the constitutional right of a state to choose its own institutions—including slavery.

The 1860 election of Abraham Lincoln as sixteenth president of the United States brought the problem to its final crisis. Many angry southerners feared that Lincoln, a northerner from Illinois, would abolish slavery. Rather than submit, they vowed to leave the Union. On December 20, 1860, South Carolina seceded from the United States. Mississippi, Florida, Alabama, Georgia, Louisiana, and Texas soon followed. Personally, Davis opposed the idea of secession. But as a loyal southerner, he resigned from the United States Senate on January 21, 1861. In his farewell address, he declared his hope for a peaceful solution to the nation's problems.

Abraham Lincoln

A map showing the states that seceded from the Union in 1861

A photograph of Davis taken just before the Civil War

However, as Varina Davis later remembered, when she and her husband left the Senate chamber, "we felt blood in the air."

Within days, delegates from the seceding states gathered at the Exchange Hotel in Montgomery, Alabama. These southern leaders quickly drafted a southern constitution. On February 9, 1861, they unanimously elected Jefferson Davis president of the brand-new Confederate States of America.

Stunned by their choice, Davis hurried to Montgomery. Cheering crowds lined the city streets on February 18, Inauguration Day. A band blared the popular tune "Dixie," which soon became the unofficial anthem of the Confederacy. At the Alabama State Capitol, fifty-three-year-old Jefferson Davis solemnly took the oath of office. "The man and the hour have met," exclaimed southern politician William Yancey. "Prosperity, honor and victory await his administration."

Davis knew that many difficulties lay ahead. The new nation, heading quickly toward war with the North, would require gallant leadership. Davis did not want war; in fact, his first act as president was to send a peace commission to Washington to prevent armed conflict. But if war became inevitable, President Davis was prepared to face the challenge. The South would be at a tremendous disadvantage. It had a population of

Jefferson Davis's inauguration at the Alabama State Capitol

only about 9 million people, while 20 million people filled the northern states. The agricultural South had almost no industry, inferior railroads, and no powder mill, army, navy, or shipyard. "We are without machinery, without means, and threatened by a powerful [enemy]," admitted Davis, "but I . . . will not shrink from the task imposed on me." Full of energy, he set about naming cabinet members, appointing military officers, and planning government policies.

The Confederates ordered all U.S. military

troops to leave the forts located in the southern states. President Lincoln, however, regarded those forts as United States property, and refused to remove the troops. On April 12, 1861, Confederate cannon opened fire upon Fort Sumter in the harbor of Charleston, South Carolina. For two days, screaming shells slammed into the fort's brick walls until the Union garrison raised a white flag.

The surrender of Fort Sumter marked the start of the Civil War. Abraham Lincoln called for 75,000 volunteers to put down the southern rebellion. In response, Virginia, North Carolina, Tennessee, and Arkansas soon left the Union to

President Davis and his cabinet

Thousands of men responded to President Lincoln's call for volunteers.

join their sister slaveholding states in the
Confederacy. "We'll hang Jeff Davis on a sour
apple tree" were the words sung loudly by
regiments of young Yankee recruits. Southerners
flocked to join the Confederate army. They
regarded the coming fight as a second war of
independence.

In June, the Confederate government moved
from Montgomery to Richmond, Virginia. The
Virginia State House became the Confederate
Capitol. The Brockenbrough House, at the
Corner of Twelfth and Clay streets, was bought
by the city to be used as the Executive Mansion.

*A badge worn
in support of
the Confederacy*

Generals P. G. T. Beauregard, Albert S. Johnston, and Joseph Johnston

Every day, President Davis walked to his offices in the old U.S. Customs House on Main Street. Two or three times a week, he gathered his cabinet for formal meetings. Davis hoped that the need for southern cotton would persuade England and France to recognize and help the Confederacy. In the meantime, he concentrated on military affairs.

Already, a blockade of Union gunboats controlled the Atlantic and Gulf seacoasts. Union armies were marching into Virginia and Tennessee. President Davis depended on such Confederate generals as P. G. T. Beauregard, Albert Sidney Johnston, and Joseph Johnston to defend southern territory.

"Richmond must not be given up—it shall not be given up," Davis exclaimed in May 1862. The war had been raging for a year, with no end in sight. By this time, the Union army of General George B. McClellan had marched to within a few miles of the Confederate capital. To make things worse, on May 31, General Joseph Johnston, commander of the Confederate forces in Virginia, was wounded in battle. Davis responded to this emergency by appointing his trusted military advisor, General Robert E. Lee, as the new commander of the Confederate Army of Northern Virginia. This move by Davis was, as one historian put it, "the best decision of his presidency." In a series of bloody attacks that came to be known as the Seven Days' Battles, Lee shocked McClellan into retreat.

Robert E. Lee

Wounded Union troops in the aftermath of one of the Seven Days' Battles

A drawing of a Confederate ten-dollar bill

As the war dragged on month after month, hard economic times hit the South. Confederate money lost its value. Clothing and food became terribly expensive. On April 2, 1863, hungry women rioted in Richmond. With hatchets and axes, they smashed windows and broke open the doors of grocery stores. Davis rushed to the scene and tried to calm the mob. Climbing atop a nearby wagon, he shouted for the crowd's attention. First he promised them food. Then he emptied his own pockets and threw what money he had to the crowd. Finally, he insisted that the women return to their homes. Armed guards now stood close at hand with guns leveled. "We do not desire to injure anyone," Davis declared, "But this lawlessness must stop." At last, the grumbling women went home. President Davis, however, was greatly distressed by the incident. It weighed heavily on him that he had little power to help these hungry, desperate women—and he knew that there were thousands of others like them throughout the South.

The tide of war turned against the South in 1863. "The clouds are truly dark over us," Davis admitted sadly. Bloodied Confederate troops surrendered Vicksburg, Mississippi. Along dusty roads they retreated from battlefields at Gettysburg, Pennsylvania; and Chattanooga, Tennessee. When Union troops again threatened Richmond on May 11, 1864, Davis himself helped rally the defense at Drewry's Bluff, outside the city. "He never appeared to greater advantage," exclaimed one Confederate officer. "Calm, self-contained, cheerful, hopeful, determined, he was an inspiration." One Federal shell crashed near the president and sent dirt flying. Calmly, Davis walked away.

In 1863, the tide of war turned against the Confederacy.

When Federal troops marched into Richmond in April 1865, much of it was in ruins from fires set by retreating Confederates.

Davis was at this church when he learned that Richmond had to be abandoned.

Though the Richmond defenses held, Union general Ulysses S. Grant ordered a siege of the city. Meanwhile, Union general William T. Sherman was marching across Georgia, burning farms and tearing up railroad tracks. By the spring of 1865, the Confederacy tottered near ruin. In the trenches outside Richmond, General Lee realized that his starving, barefoot soldiers could not hold out much longer. Gloom spread over the city. At the end of March, Davis sent Varina and their children south in search of greater safety.

On Sunday, April 2, Davis sat in his pew at St. Paul's Episcopal Church. A messenger quietly walked down the aisle and handed the president a paper. When Davis opened it, he learned

General Lee's latest news. The enemy had broken through his lines. His shaken army would have to retreat that night. Davis rose, put on his overcoat, and silently left the church. Anxious people followed after him. Rumors buzzed through the streets that Richmond must be abandoned.

Through the next hurried hours, Davis and his aides packed personal papers and government documents. The president had decided that he and his cabinet must escape from the doomed city. At 11:00 P.M., he climbed aboard a train heading south. On April 9, General Lee surrendered his army to Union general Ulysses S.

General Lee's surrender at Appomattox on April 9, 1865

Grant near Appomattox Court House, Virginia. In spite of this shock, Davis defiantly told loyal Confederates, "The cause is not yet dead." He hoped to make it west of the Mississippi River and continue leading the fight from Texas. In truth, however, the entire Confederacy had collapsed. "Poor President [Davis]," realized one Virginia private, "he is unwilling to see what all around him see."

The United States government offered a reward of $100,000 for Davis's capture. On horseback, Davis fled into Georgia with a few dozen of his most loyal followers. On May 6, he caught up

Davis and his followers fleeing southward after Lee's surrender

$100,000 REWARD! IN GOLD.

Head Quarters Cav. Corp.,
Military Division Mississippi,
Macon Ga., May 6, 1865.

One Hundred Thousand Dollars Reward

in Gold, will be paid to any person or persons who will apprehend and deliver JEFFERSON DAVIS to any of the Military authorities of the United States.

Several millions of specie, reported to be with him, will become the property of the captors.

J. H. WILSON

A U.S. government poster offering a reward for Davis's capture

with the wagons carrying his wife and children. He vowed to himself to protect them from danger while he could. Four days later, at Irwinville, Union cavalrymen surrounded the little camp. In the confusion of the attack, Davis made one last effort to escape. Alert troopers soon pointed their rifles at him, however. As Varina rushed to his side, Davis realized he must at last surrender.

The Yankee soldiers grinned when they learned that they had captured the hated Jefferson Davis. Rumors swiftly spread that Davis had been wearing women's clothes when he was captured. By accident, in the the morning darkness, he had grabbed his wife's rain cape instead of his own.

The clothing Davis was wearing when captured

A steamship carried the prisoner up the Atlantic coast to Fortress Monroe, Virginia. Davis spent the next 720 days locked within its thick brick walls. During his first week in prison, guards fixed leg irons to his ankles. "Our beloved President is in chains," moaned one southern woman when she learned the news. Many northerners demanded that Davis be hanged for treason. Month after month, the proud Confederate suffered in his cramped cell. To heal the wounds of war, President Andrew Johnson granted pardons to thousands of Confederates willing to take an oath of allegiance to the United States. Davis stubbornly refused to take such an oath.

At last, on May 13, 1867, New York newspaper publisher Horace Greeley and several other important northerners put up $100,000 bail for Davis's release. Set free in Richmond, Davis still hoped for his day in court. But the United States never brought him to trial. For a time, Davis lived in Canada and Europe. Old and gray, he returned at last to Mississippi. During the war, many southerners had complained about Davis's leadership. In these later years, however, they grew to admire him as a brave symbol of the South's "Lost Cause."

Jefferson Davis died in New Orleans on December 6, 1889, at the age of eighty-one. Throughout the South, from Virginia to Texas,

Jefferson Davis, surrounded by members of his family, at home in Mississippi in the 1880s

bells tolled and cannon boomed. Mourning southerners laid his body to final rest in Richmond, Virginia, the scene of so many of his triumphs and trials. "The past is dead; let it bury its dead," old Jefferson Davis had urged his countrymen. From the ashes of the Civil War, the South was rising once again to become a proud and powerful part of the United States.

INDEX

PHOTO CREDITS

Cover, The Museum of the Confederacy, Richmond/Katherine Wetzel; Museum of the City of New York, New York/
Fort Sumpter, Currier and Ives/Art Resource, New York; 1, National Portrait Gallery, Washington, D.C./Art Resource,
New York; 2, The Museum of the Confederacy, Richmond Virginia, Photography by Katherine Wetzel; 4, Eleanor S.
Brockenbrough Library, The Museum of the Confederacy, Richmond, Virginia; 5, Historical Pictures/Stock Montage; 6,
Transylvania University; 7 (top), West Point Museum Collections; 7 (bottom), North Wind; 8 (both photos), Historical
Pictures/Stock Montage; 9, North Wind; 10, Eleanor S. Brockenbrough Library, The Museum of the Confederacy; 11,
Historical Pictures/Stock Montage; 12, North Wind; 13, 14, Historical Pictures/Stock Montage; 15, 16 (both photos),
North Wind; 17 (top), Library of Congress; 17 (bottom), North Wind; 18, AP/Wide World; 19, North Wind; 20, Eleanor S.
Brockenbrough Library, The Museum of the Confederacy; 21 (both photos), North Wind; 22 (left), AP/Wide World; 22
(center), Historical Pictures/Stock Montage; 22 (right), Museum of the Confederacy/Courtesy National Archives; 23
(top), Museum of the Confederacy/Courtesy Virginia Historical Society; 23 (bottom), AP/Wide World; 24, 25, North
Wind; 26 (top), AP/Wide World; 26 (bottom), Museum of the Confederacy/Courtesy Library of Congress; 27, Historical
Pictures/Stock Montage; 28, 29 (top), North Wind; 29 (bottom), Historical Pictures/Stock Montage; 31, Beauvoir/Library
of Congress/Courtesy of Mississippi Department of Archives and History

Picture Identifications:

Page 1: A photograph of Jefferson Davis from about 1858
Page 2: An oil portrait of Jefferson Davis by John P. Walker

Project Editor: Shari Joffe
Designer: Karen Yops
Photo Editor: Jan Izzo
Cornerstones of Freedom Logo: David Cunningham

ABOUT THE AUTHOR

Zachary Kent grew up in Little Falls, New Jersey, and received a degree in English from St. Lawrence
University. After college, he worked at a New York City literary agency for two years and then launched
his writing career. Mr. Kent has had a lifelong interest in American history. Studying the presidents was
his childhood hobby.